Meta-Reflections:
16 Philosophical and Practical Keys to Personal Growth

Joshua Douglas Cartwright

Published by Living Words

ACKNOWLEDGMENTS

If you don't enjoy this book blame my wife ☺. She has unfailingly encouraged me to write it with all the love and understanding a good woman can give.

She thinks I have something to say on personal development that you would want to read. Something from a man who has come from a background where, if it were not for my faith in God and the use of some excellent self-help material I would have gone mad or killed someone – or myself. But I didn't go mad. I survived and prospered.

I've been using personal development materials for 20 years, coaching professionally for four, and writing about personal development for nearly three years. I've written over 100 articles during that time detailing what I've learned.

What you get in this book are my hard-won insights on the various obstacles to personal change I have encountered and overcome.

How do you know if any of them will help <u>you</u>? Well, you don't – but thousands of people have read these chapters before, - when they were articles. I know at least some of them benefitted people because of the comments they left.

I'm not offering a one-step manifesto to instant change. I'm also not saying this is the last self-help book you'll never need. I am saying that I think you will find something in here that will get you thinking and acting in a new way – and them my job will be done. If you find two things – even better. So if you benefit from something in this book – thank my wife. It's all her fault.

Index

Chapter 1 - Personal Development: An Essential Key

Chapter 2 - De-Personalising personal development

Chapter 3 - The (re)acquistion of your personal power

Chapter 4 – Fixed Versus Growth

Chapter 5 - Real Change: Should it be this uncomfortable?

Chapter 6 - Want real change? This time it's personal

Chapter 7 – Meaning: the cornerstone of personal development

Chapter 8 - Three Words that kill the Human Spirit

Chapter 9 – broken trolley: unsound mind

Chapter 10 - BRING IT ON to win it

Chapter 11 - An argument for Optimism

Chapter 12 – The number one key for managing your Emotions

Chapter 13 – When pleasure becomes a Pain

Chapter 14 - Great idea: - but can you feel it?

Chapter 15 - A new philosophy about failure

Chapter 16 - Increasing focus with the power of intention

Chapter 1 - Personal Development: An Essential Key

Is there an essential key to personal development? One without which the unlocking of your potential might be difficult - if not impossible?

If we define personal development as growth involving the mind and the body, then yes – I think there is.

Without this key personal growth is slow, and sluggish. Without learning how to tap into this essential human 'tool', change will be sporadic or imposed from the outside.

And I believe the really important part is this: without developing this function of consciousness, **all** deep change will be difficult.

It does not matter what courses you buy, which 'gurus' you listen to, how many self-growth seminars you take. Because this is one thing you cannot do without: The ability to self-observe, what some people call *self-awareness*.

Self-awareness meaning the ability to become aware of what is going on in:

* Your mind's eye (the cinema screen of your mind)

* Your inner ear (verbal self-talk, sounds, talk from other 'parts' of you)

* Your feelings (meaning and feelings inside and on the outside of your body)

* Your emotions (feelings that you have labelled as 'emotions')

* Your intuition- literally your 'inner-knowing'

If you are not aware of what is going on inside YOU – what your perceptions are reporting to you on the inside you lack access to vital information. It's like sitting in a sport's car without a key to the engine - or being locked in first gear.

You can't change what you're not aware of.

According to the National Autistic Society UK 65% of the population predominantly think using their visual system. Yet a common complaint for people trying to learn how to use performance improvement technologies like Neuro-Linguistic Programming (NLP) is: "I just don't see pictures in my head."

Actually, they do - they are just not aware of them.

But since so much of that field's techniques use the questions: "Imagine that…" or "Remember a time when…" it is useful to understand some ways of accessing that information. Even if you just want to have more access to using your visual imagination you need to increase your awareness of those pictures.

The most powerful way I have found (and I've been using it since at least 2001) is *Image Streaming* by Win Wenger. http://www.winwenger.com/ebooks.htm

This is a process of describing out-loud anything you are aware of in your mind's eye (and I mean anything, even blips of light), and it offers numerous methods for kick-starting a 'stream' of images in your awareness.

I've found that people who 'can't see images' report 'break-throughs' to 'seeing' in only a few minutes, thereby automatically increasing their access to their perceptions and self-insight (literally in-sight!)

My metaphor for using this technique is it's like clearing out a partially blocked drain. At one end is the unconscious mind that wants to push answers and ideas through to the consciousness. But this conduit is blocked by rust (lack of use!). Image streaming allows you to receive more information from your incredibly powerful, God-given, unconscious mind.

Another way to develop the sharpness of mental images – if you already see blurry or indistinct images – is to use the snapshot method.

Quite simply, look at something like a rose or a car and 'snapshot it': close your eyes and describe as much of what you see in your mind's eye as you can. Use only sensory words: I see…red…the flowers have green stems with triangular thorns…there is a white picket fence behind them…". Then open your eyes and compare what you saw inside with what you see outside. This has the effect of sharpening your visual memory as well.

Benefits

Why <u>would</u> you put so much effort into becoming aware of your perceptions?

Well, if you like ancient advice, the Temple of Apollo at Delphi supposedly had "know thyself" over the door. And if you have habits you want to change then you often need to find what's making them tick. You need to "know thyself" and what makes you tick at a whole deeper level.

The famous Gestalt therapist Fritz Perls said, "Awareness *per se* is curative". What does this mean? Think about it – have you ever realised something you didn't know you thought, and exclaimed : "That's stupid! I can't believe I thought that" – and it was gone? That's what he meant!

The realisation or flash of insight itself can be the catalyst for the change!

An added bonus is (and I saved the best for last) Image Streaming offers an *increase in measurable intelligence.*

Win Wenger had tests of image streamers conducted by Charles P. Reinert at South West State University and found that there were nearly ½ point of measurable IQ increase for every hour of use and an average of 9 point increase after 20.5 hours of use (http://www.vth.biz/kb/html.php?category=10#category-10

- CTRL+F and search for '**Reinert**').

Now, most of us know that nowadays intelligence is not considered to just measurable with linguistic and mathematical abilities – Howard Gardner writes about *Multiple Intelligences* including visio-spatial, musical and kinaesthetic intelligence.

But Image Streaming can help with **all** of these.

I've personally used it to solve problems, get insights, create new techniques and improve as a coach.

In fact, Win Wenger has produced a kit with Paul Scheele of *PhotoReading* fame called *The Genius Code*. It has all the directions you need to tap into your ever-flowing unconscious yet brilliant Image Stream.

If you are starting at the beginning I understand it can be frustrating to have to build awareness little by little each day. But before long you will make a quantum leap and your self-awareness will show you things you never knew about yourself and your potential.

Chapter 2 - De-Personalising personal development

Here's a thought that might spin your head.

Personal development is not personal! It's not about you.

It IS personal in that what you 'personally develop' is particular to your beliefs, your skills, and your situation – but it's not about the 'you' who is unconditionally valuable and beyond judgment.

I said it would spin your head. But stick with me, there is good news to come.

Some words in the English language are what are called in linguistic studies – multi-ordinal. This means that the same word means different things in different contexts. This is easily understood when you consider that saying: 'I love you' to your fluffy cute dog or cat is not the same as saying it to your husband or wife in bed. It's the same word, different context and hence different meanings.

So why is this good news for you and your personal development?

It's good news if you are someone who personalises comments, who feels that you're being talked about, that you have to have your radar always on in case someone says something bad about you.

If you are someone who says, "'I failed" and feels bad about yourself rather than just not getting the result you want, it could be because you are confusing the levels of 'you' that does something with the you that is beyond judgement.

This might help to explain it. NLP pioneer Robert Dilts created a model called the Neuro-logical levels which suggested that we think in 'levels' and making a change at the higher levels impact what we perceive at the lower ones. Hence a change at the level of mission could affect how we see ourselves (Identity).

Here's the complete list:

· Mission

· Identity
· Values
· Beliefs
· Capabilities
· Behavior
· Environment

You will also notice that Identity - who you ARE - is at a different level to Capabilities and Behavior – what you DO.

It's good news because *you are not what you do*. It's not about YOU (Identity). Despite what the people around you say.

As a Meta-Coach, I find that when my clients have linked judgements about their performance with judgements about their personal worth it creates a yo-yo effect (good performance = I'm worthwhile, bad performance = I'm a worthless person). It also hinders people from taking the actions and risks they need in order to progress. They feel that the essential core of who they ARE is being threatened. The part that is 'I', the part that is 'me' doesn't want to be changed.

But who or <u>what</u> is 'I'?

Try this. Say to yourself, "**I** have feelings, but **I** am not my feelings. . .my feelings change but **I** remain . . .**I** have beliefs but **I** am not my beliefs. . .my beliefs change but **I** remain . . .**I** have a body but **I** am not my body. . .my body changes but **I** remain."

Emphasize the '**I**' when you speak, accent it more heavily. It has a strange effect, doesn't it?

So if 'I' am not any of these things…then what am I?

Many say "I think, therefore I am."

Here is my perspective.

I'm a Christian and I believe that God created me and put His life in me. That life is unconditionally valuable and cannot be devalued. That is what constitutes 'I' for me.

I also believe that He gave me the kind of consciousness that enables me to think about myself and all aspects of myself.

Thus, – you might want to read this twice – the thinker (which is me/I) is not the same as what is thought about – my thoughts. It, like identity and behavior in Robert's model are different phenomena of me.

So for me 'I' is a spiritual issue, and I (and it/my value) am separate from what I think. "I am – therefore I think".

I know others will have different ideas and we each have to choose what we base our understanding of ourselves on.

What I have done is take on a concept of 'I' that is not affected by the judgments that are made about what I do. And because I accept that God values me I don't have to convince myself that I am valuable simply because I say so…

How would this idea of 'I' have unconditional value work for you if you did it?

For one, this makes it much easier to pick up the phone and have my ideas rejected rather than my 'self' rejected.

And concerning 'failure' (which is another one of those 'multi-ordinal words.) if you fail, what exactly failed?

Was it YOU – the entire mind body system that supposedly constitutes who you are?

Did your mind shut down?
Did your blood stop pumping?

- Did your immune system shut down?
  Did your muscles atrophy?
  Did your throat muscles die?
- Did those things 'fail'?

Because that is what you are saying if 'I' am my thoughts-body.

Was it the YOU that remains *even if* your beliefs and values change? (I stopped believing in Santa at least two years ago).

Or is it just that your mental blueprint for doing something was incomplete or inaccurate?

You had a missing piece of knowledge or something you knew was out-of-date.

Would that be so bad? After all, databases need updating, don't they? We've all had letters for previous tenants or mail with our name misspelled.

I like to think of my thoughts as tools. Along with my understanding and application of my faith, I want my mind and body to serve me.

Distinguishing 'I' as director and overseer from the 'I' who thinks and acts may seem a little schizophrenic to some.

But if you consider that since the economic recession started there have been several high profile suicides of very rich people who lost a lot of money – and who may have connected some important aspect of self with the amount of money they had – maybe separating worth and doing, worth and possessions is not such a bad idea after all.

Jesus said: "A man's life does not consist of his possessions."

So – do you still think that if I get something wrong the failure is about my worth?

Is personal development still personal?

Look me in the 'I' and say that.

Chapter 3 - the (re)acquistion of your personal power

Power: *What a subject.*

We all desire power to varying degrees whether we call it 'power' or 'control' or something else. Whether or not it's power over ourselves or power over others, power to do good, power to do evil, power to create, power to destroy, we are fascinated by the subject.

We write about it

*"Power tends to corrupt, and absolute power corrupts absolutely." -**Lord Acton***

We sing about it.

*"I got the power!" -**Snap***

We study those who exercise it in one form or another.

*"The new ruler must determine all the injuries that he will need to inflict. He must inflict them once and for all." – **Niccolo Machiavelli***

Ultimately, despite all this attention paid, there is one foundational 'power' – that many of us lack and want and need more of.

Need a clue? Read the following quotes.

"He who controls others may be powerful, but he who has mastered himself is mightier still"

Lao Tzu quotes (Chinese Taoist Philosopher, founder of Taoism, 600 BC-531 BC)

"Most powerful is he who has himself in his own power."

Seneca (5 BC – 65 AD)

It is, of course, one's *personal power*.

Your personal power relates how to how much you are able to consciously use your tools of consciousness:

Thinking: (**T**) Mental frames about beliefs, decisions, expectations, values and thinking strategies etc

Emoting (E): Your visceral feelings with added mental labels. We can feel a feeling in the body and name it anger, joy , sadness etc - but we can also have 'meta-feelings' which have no specific location: self-esteem, proactivity, courage etc

Speaking(S): The words, non-verbal sounds that come out of our mouths

Behaving(B): Your actions, direction of motor skills etc.

If you don't feel like you own your own (T-E-S-B), if you feel out of control, if you feel like others push your buttons, if you are a people pleaser, a scut-monkey for the desires of others , then you lack the *perception* that your personal power is your own.

The truth is you *never* lack personal power. You simply lack *awareness* that it already is yours and already is under your control. You just don't believe it.

Think through the logic.

Every day you use your T-E-S-B to get up, go to work, speak to friends, argue with shop assistants, and make dinner. You think about what you will and won't do, feel what you feel and either vent or take deep breathes.

You already use what you think you don't have.

So the issue is not, <u>not having</u> the power, but rather you *perceive* or *feel* like you can't or don't have power at certain times and in certain places:

Our attention gets diverted by our beliefs about what we can and cannot do, by the strength of **our** reactions to the reactions of other people.

What drives these reactions?

I want to say first that I spent YEARS looking for ways to feel more powerful in myself. Years of my life, thousands of hours, thousands of pounds, and more self-help junk than I could give away.

But I discovered that one of the most basic reasons for feeling powerless is feeling not worthy as a person, and feeling not able to cope with what life throws at us.

When we don't feel worthy as a human being, when we feel we are bad, like we don't have the right to exist, like we are nothing, there is almost no greater pain.

We spend our time worrying about what others think but the truth is that we are worrying what WE think about ourselves. We exercise what power we think we have protecting ourselves from ourselves and what we think others think!

I find a lot of people in self-help circles don't believe in God as the Bible describes Him, so I'm going to keep this simple.

I do. And believing that He created me in His own image, that what He created (me) is **"very good"** (Gen 1:27). Thus, I have an inward affirmation of an outward perception of my Value from Someone who knows. And I am very secure about my Value.

However, whilst I wish more people would believe in God, it is not necessary to do so in order to believe in your value. You can believe in the unconditional worth of human beings *per* se and set that frame about your Self.

Doing so tends to remove the worry about your worth because you are *esteeming* yourself.

And when you're not worrying about your self worth, you can concentrate on the next part, which is the using your 'tools of consciousness.'

Susan Jeffers, author of *Feel the Fear and Do it Anyway*, says that the number one fear we have is the fear of not being able to cope.

The field of Neuro-Linguistic-Programming teaches an assumption that we have all the resources we need to do what we need to do.

Therefore, we all have the brain power, muscle tone, voice boxes, and mental imagery to reaffirm that we ARE in control.

Personal power involves taking that assumption and exercising self-control, taking responsibility for your response-ability, and being accountable FOR yourself and TO your relationships with others.

This all starts with (re)acknowledging ownership over our God-given tools of consciousness.

How can we do this?

One effective way is with the Neurosemantics Ownership Pattern. You can get it as part of the Personal PowerPack from www.personal-powerpack.com

"One person with a belief is equal to a force of 99 who have only interests."

John Stuart Mill (1806 – 1873)

I will give you a taste, however, of what ownership feels like:

What do you feel is totally yours?

What is so yours that no-one could take away from you?

Imagine feeling that strongly about your thoughts.

Or imagine a time when you were about to say something harsh but you paused, thought, and decided to say something different.

That's an example of using your personal power.

There are a great deal of different reasons why people don't feel worthy enough to use their personal power.

One reason we don't feel esteemed and don't feel in control comes from historical factors involving our upbringing and lack of positive affirmation from parents and others.

But it doesn't have to stay that way. If you are prepared to hear it, those memories exist **today** with a date stamp of five, ten and more years on them. Would you keep canned food that long? So why do you keep out of date memories that long?

We don't have to live out of old frames of reference any more. How does it help you at 25 to be using the thinking of a 7 year old? Yet that is how many people feel and what they do.

I challenge you not to stay this way. Challenge what seems to be true, what seems to be real where feeling 'out of control' is concerned. Get angry and change. Or get someone else to help you do it. If you're going to change any part of the world, you often need to change yourself first.

Chapter 4 - Fixed Versus Growth

"It's not how hard you can hit. It's how hard you can *get hit* and keep on moving forward."

Rocky Balboa.

What is a key difference between those who dust themselves off and keep 'moving forward' after one of life's 'hits' and those who drop like a stone?

It's not possible in one article to cover all of the reasons people struggle to move forward. (although that didn't stop Americans spending 13 million on personal development in 2010 trying to find out!). However, as dedicated psychologists and sociologists increasingly investigate subjects like happiness and optimism (Seligman), genius and talent (Dweck), procrastination (Steel) and influence (Cialdini) they are uncovering significant keys or leverage points which can make our lives more effective and fruitful.

One such key exists in the difference between a **growth** and a **fixed** mindset. I will be borrowing liberally from Mindset by Carol S. Dweck as well as other literature to explain the importance of this.

Here's a promise: Understanding and implementing this distinction can liberate you to embrace growth as your birthright. It may also deal with a host of negative consequences that come with using the fixed mindset. But more on that later.

So what is a fixed mindset?

Basically, a fixed mindset believes you have some quality or you don't. You're good at something or you're not. You're smart or you're not. You're beautiful or you're not.

So what, you say? It's true. Some of us have inborn talent and some don't. It's obvious. Just look in the playground for example–some kids are good at football and some are not.

Only… a reading of books like <u>The Talent Code</u>, <u>Bounce</u>, and <u>Talent is Overrated</u> strongly suggest that its not so. They looked at so-called geniuses (and also at the places in the world that produce exceptional talent) and concluded that an outrageous amount of the right kind of practice is really what separated the goods from the greats. In other words, anyone who works hard enough and applies themselves to developing skills the 'right' way can develop what looks and smells like genius.

"Well, maybe" so you say – "but I <u>was</u> born with an advantage. I was good at music/sport/board-surfing since an early age."

I'm not God, perhaps you were. But let's look at the dangers of assuming you have fixed inborn talent or smarts. I have heard of 'smart' children who go to schools for gifted pupils and suddenly find themselves surrounded with others far 'smarter' than themselves. Or so it seems.

What are they to think? This is where the difference between the fixed and growth mindsets starts to kick in.

Children with the fixed mindset start to doubt that they are that talented or smart after all. They are surrounded by kids who really seem to have 'it', to have been touched by God.

Tracking studies have shown that children with this mindset fall behind in their grades after two years. They increasingly tend to avoid situations they think they can't handle thus *avoiding the opportunity to grow.*

Project that avoidance tendency over a lifetime and you get a lifetime of under-achieving on your full potential.

Children with the growth mindset understand already that <u>they can learn from those who know more than them</u>. They believe they can get that good through learning and practice.

They may seek out extra help. They may befriend people with a greater talent and find out 'how they do it.'

They actually relish challenges because what they see is the growth, not that the challenge means there's something wrong with them.

Let me let you in on the secret. Growth oriented people don't focus on the *hit*, they focus on the *moving forward.*

Fixed mindset people focus on what the hit means about *them.*

> Dweck says "From the point of view of people with the fixed mindset, effort is only for people with deficiencies. And when people already know they're deficient, they have nothing to loose by trying. But if your claim to fame is not having any deficiencies – if you're a genius, a talent, or a natural – then you have a lot to loose.
>
> Effort can *reduce* you." p42

What develops the fixed mindset?

Ironically, praising or criticizing a child for having (or lacking) a particular quality can start the problem. It seems more natural and easier to tell a child (like my 18 month old) "You're so smart" when she brings me my toothbrush and exclaims "daddy teeth" . This could encourage the fixed mindset whereas "I'm so pleased you worked that out – that you brush your teeth with the toothbrush" encourages effort and further thinking.

So what keeps the fixed mindset in place?

Lack of awareness of the growth mindset is one reason!

But now you're learning about it your mind, stretched by a new idea, will never go back to its original dimensions (thanks Oliver Wendell Holmes for the quote!)

Secondly, because of the way our minds look for evidence for what we already believe if we see the world through 'some have it, some don't' eyes we'll continue to do so unless we have a jolt that forces us to re-evaluate.

Here's a jolt: if you have a *fixed* mindset you can kiss long-term high self-esteem good-bye. Why?

Because each time there's a challenge to how smart and talented you are your self-esteem (which is based on this) is threatened.

Even if you overcome there can always be the lurking suspicion and fear about what will happen if you fail. You won't be smart. Then what WILL you be? A loser?

Do you really want to think like that? Many do.

But the cost of such thinking is anxiety, avoidance, lack of growth, despair, self-criticism, unfulfilled potential blah, blah, yadah, yadah!

Now before you fall into a pit of despair I want to reassure you that there are ways to ameliorate this mindset.

As mentioned above, just learning about the new mindset can create a shift towards growth thinking.

Dweck reports one child who, having realised that intelligence was not fixed, asked with tears in his eyes: "So I don't have to be dumb?" From that moment on he improved greatly in his attitude and grades.

If you're very self-critical you need to create a framework of self-acceptance, appreciation and esteem. If you struggle with this The Personal PowerPack available from Amazon can help you set these frames.

If you have a fixed mindset you may overuse a mental process called Identification.

Alfred Korzybski, creator of General Semantics, talked about the **unsanity** of identification. Although this sounds technical it refers to how we make linkages in our minds between things.

When we make links between who we are and a negative idea we can mentally imprison ourselves. For example, the belief 'I AM a loser gets mentally processed as 'I' = LOSER.

Your mind will equate EVERYTHING you are with the idea of LOSER. Except you're not a whole and total looser, are you? Are you?

Are you not more expansive and complicated and wonderful than that? I hope you think so.

Take a piece of paper and write out answers to:

I am a...................

Then ask yourself if those descriptions say everything about you? Really? You're just a x? In every situation? At all times?

If you're having trouble changing beliefs you can use something like the Reboot Your Mind CD at www.change-my-beliefs.com a radical belief change process which can free up your mind when you feel 'stuck' in a certain mindset.

How can you change from a fixed mindset to a growth mindset? (full details on http://www.mindsetonline.com)

1) Learn to hear your fixed mindset voice

As you hit a setback, the voice might say, "This would have been a snap if you really had talent." "You see, I told you it was a risk. Now you've gone and shown the world how limited you are." " It's not too late to back out, make excuses, and try to regain your dignity.

2) Recognize that you have a choice

You can interpret challenges as a sign that your fixed talent or abilities are lacking. Or you can interpret them with a growth mindset as a sign you need to make extra effort, find new strategies and stretch yourself.

3) Talk back to it with a growth mindset

So many personal issues never change because we don't think to challenge them.

You need to challenge your fixed mindset with a new growth frame of mind.

So, ' my taxes are too difficult' with 'I can handle this by taking it slowly – one concept at a time. Each section mastered is a step forward, I've learned something new and I'm improving.

Even just telling yourself: "Plenty of people have learned how to do this. I can learn this too and improve as I go."

4) Take growth mindset action

Do something that reflects your new growth mindset.

The final word is this: a growth mind set helps you become MORE of who you truly are. A fixed mindset immobilizes you and fossilizes your natural growth abilities inside a cocoon of having to prove yourself.

Go out and grow!

Chapter 5 - Real Change: Should it be this uncomfortable?

"Tension and discomfort are necessary feelings in the process of achieving your goal. In fact, if you do not experience them then the goal is not important or not what you really want."

Cognitive Behavioral Therapy, Avy Joseph (p114)

Marines train their minds to over-ride the pain impulses of their bodies. They can survive under torture, and out in harsh terrain in ways that would kill the rest of us.

People have willingly died for their beliefs – and survived because of them.

Victor Frankl got through a German concentration camp in horrific conditions because he believed there was something worth living for on the other side. He faced beatings, starvation and disease to extremes we can barely imagine.

This means that pain *can* be experienced to an outrageous degree but the people involved managed to live, get through it, and do what they needed to do to achieve their mission, or make it to the end of their confinement.

We in the West live in a society where life is easy compared to most of the rest of the world. We medicate ourselves every time we feel a twinge, and dose ourselves with food, sex, drugs, and entertainment whenever we feel unhappy.

We run away from discomfort and tell ourselves we can't stand the problems in our lives. See the examples above. As if we really know what problems are!

As Avy Joseph says:

"We all experience problems in many areas of our lives but don't always realise that our minds and bodies respond to how we rate them. Evaluating a difficulty as <u>*unbearable*</u> *is not only flawed but*

it also triggers images and feeling that fight against goal achievement (p31)"

I think we think we shouldn't have to experience pain on the way to our success. Think again!

If you've ever watched the violent and satirical sci-fi film Starship Troopers you'll see the drill sergeant spear a recruit's hand with a knife and then announce as the recruit screams, "PAIN – is in your mind." I think it probably felt quite real to the person with the knife through his hand!

Nevertheless, the idea is that it's not just the feeling but what you tell yourself about it that determines whether you'll get through it. In other words, it's the meanings we choose to give to our discomfort.

Why we don't stick with change

We tell ourselves that we *can't stand* the feelings that come with it as if the feelings shouldn't be there. I know. I did this for years.

Here's a revelation I had which is changing my life:

Those *'feelings'* are **completely** normal. Yes, completely.

They are as normal as hunger when you haven't eaten, sadness when you lose something valuable to you, and breathing hard if you've run a lot. They are as much a part of you as sexual desire (although we don't usually enjoy them as much!).

They're <u>hot-wired</u> into your mind-body system so they're not going anywhere anytime soon.

All this time you may have been rejecting the natural tensions that come along with changing the status quo. Isn't that kind of like hating yourself for breathing?

This is partly why Susan Jeffers said, "Feel the fear and do it anyway." The *fear seems* like a stop sign but is actually just neurological-kinesthetic information, It tells you you are measuring your perceptions of the gap between what you <u>have</u>, and what you <u>want</u>.

But the experts say we are engineered for change. So why **do** we feel tense and uncomfortable?

Well, the simple explanation is this. Your mind is designed to reinforce what you *already* believe. It has too, or you could not live a life where you doubted every element of your existence. If you did, you could not function. You'd be too scared to step out of bed in the morning in case the floor ate you. Or the bed!

So when you attempt to change, your mind and body resists. It sends out waves of discomfort. It says, "Stop! The status quo is under threat." This, is completely natural.

And maybe you have stopped. Too often?

But now you KNOW those feelings are natural, they're just part of the process of change where <u>old</u> beliefs fight for their existence, you have the first piece of what you need. I don't deny that this is a hard piece of truth. But it is true.

If you believe that God made you, then you believe that every part of you that is made is good for purpose, even if we don't always use it that way or feel it so. If you believe you just evolved, then these signals are simply that – *signals* from a body and mind about itself and its environment. They're not instructions, and I genuinely don't think they're an infallible guidance system as some personal development writers suggest. If they are, mine must be broken...!

So if we are often going to feel uncomfortable with the process of change (and I acknowledge there are plenty of times when change is fun) then what will help us stick with it until the change is made?

A goal we passionately value and want
Healthy beliefs
Healthy self-talk
Reasons to persevere

Exercise

So what is the thing you want to change? What will the outcome be when you have got it?

What difference is the change going to make in the 'real' world that is worth fighting for? How will I know I am different when I have made the change? What will be the improvements in my attitude and performance.

Grab a piece of paper write it down.

Now ask yourself what you currently think about making that change. Write down all the worries, fears, gripes and 'I can't' statements.

The next thing to do is to create a healthy belief about these feelings. It helps to write out a paragraph of what you want to believe instead.

(Avy Joseph says a healthy belief is *what you want plus keeping it real* (p98). An unhealthy belief usually demands the world 'must' and 'should' conform to its demands.)

Let's say that you were struggling to overcome your feelings. Let's say your goal is to experience the a firm grip on your remote control of power. Why a remote control? Well, if you hold it – no-one can push your buttons! You have some idea of what it will be like to see, hear and feel that.

Think of something that upsets you. What negative or toxic thoughts do you have about that situation?

For example, do you feel you 'can't stand' to feel helpless or frustrated about something?

After writing your negative thoughts:

Re-write them to statements like "I don't love but I can stand. . .feeling helpless (for instance) ", or, "I have the power to choose to feel . .solution focused and resourceful."

You can also add in statements like "perhaps difficult but not unbearable" or "in a different category from the comfortable emotions" or "they are discomfortable messengers to prod me to alertness or to pay attention to something in my experience. "

What you have done here is given new meanings to the feelings you had and used statements to acknowledge your ownership and control of the meanings you use.

Next, you will need to make a list of what you'll get if you use the healthy belief as a reminder to push through the uncomfortable feelings – until they change.

Write out as many benefits as possible, such as:
I'll be more in control.
I'll feel more empowered.
I'll be able to go on that date.
I will ask that owner for referrals
I'll have more peace.

Now, you are armed and ready to go. You can repeat and affirm to yourself your new belief in the mirror. Claude Hopkins in *The Magic of Believing* recommends when you feel like you need reasons to go on, read your reasons to go on!

When your self talk criticizes you, take it down pro-wrestling style! Albert Ellis in his wonderful book: *How to Stubbornly Refuse to Make Yourself Miserable About Anything Ever Again – Yes Anything!* says you really need to passionately and aggressively dispute your inner talk.

Think about a couple having a humdinger of an argument. Then have it with your self-talk.

"Really?"
"According to WHO?"
"You and whose army?"
"Oh! So I have to feel helpless. Who decided that? Me. Well, I can decide OTHERWISE can't I?"

I like to think of changing the things that make us stuck as psychological 'knots.' To undo a really gnarly knot may involve a lot of huffing, puffing, walking away in disgust and coming back again with a renewed determination. Changing your meanings and beliefs can sometimes be like this.

Persevere and you'll get there. And when you've made a really good shift in meaning *remember* what it feels like – and use that memory as a reference point. Making changes is an ACTIVE process, which I find so many people don't realize. You need to pay attention to what is going on in your mind and body, and store up successes for later use – when you once again feel like you can't change.

Chapter 6 - want real change? this time it's personal

Previously, I wrote that personal development was not personal in that it was not about YOU: the inherently valuable aspect of you that is beyond definition and peoples' critical judgement. Some call it Spirit: I call it the divine spark of life that God put in you.

But if you want a secret to the successful use of the personal development materials you are using – here it is:

You need to *personalise* the change you want to make for yourself.

A little later I'm going to show you a very powerful method of doing so.

I want to briefly define 'implementation.' Implementation is where you make the things you were planning actually happen. It's where the rubber hits the road. It's where you start pedalling and the chain gets engaged and you go somewhere. Only for some of us, we pedal and the bike doesn't move because the chain's come off.

Why might this be? Let's go back to childhood for a minute (We won't stop long).

Have you ever seen any normal child suffering from lack of motivation to explore and implement? There is a reason we move objects off the low shelves, cover plug holes and use rubber door stoppers.

What I'm trying to say is that we naturally want to learn by doing and by doing so we naturally learn. We play, and we learn. To alter a phrase by the great inventor Thomas Edison (who made the light-bulb and telegraph) we are not squeamish about exploring because we realise that all of life is a great experiment.

Have you ever seen a two year old <u>not</u> wanting to try something new out? So what happens as they grow up? Well, it varies but for many people their natural curiosity gets blunted by adult indignation: "Don't touch that!" "No".

I'm not saying it's all our parents' fault (although I did go through that phase) but that older people around us, mostly because of their own problems and lack of nurturing, tell us things we believe because we don't know any better. And those things are usually limiting and toxic.

If the ability to implement could be thought of as a conduit from mind-to-muscle then for many of us it is clogged up worse than the kitchen sink. If you keep tipping 'yuk' down a sink eventually the water won't go anywhere. If you keep stifling the desire to take action that comes from great thoughts, neither will you…!

What does it really mean to 'know' something?

Here in the West we seem to have a strange delusion about what it means to 'know' something.

In the Ancient Far East the Aramaic speaking peoples' word for 'know' meant a simultaneous combination of thinking and doing. This is well expressed by a statement of Jesus who said to the people around him: "If you are truly my disciples (learners and followers) then you will obey my teachings. Then you will know the truth and the truth will set you free." (John 8:31-32)

Pick that apart a bit. Essentially Jesus said: When you take the actions and think the way I command you to do, that doing will reveal the truth to you. And then the truth that you now know (because you experienced it) *will set you free*. No doing, no experiencing – no real knowledge – and no truth or freedom.

Some of us Westerners, when asked about a subject we are familiar with, say, "I know *that*" – and we mean, "I've memorised a fact about it". But I suspect, if you have been into personal development for a while, that you know a few people who can tell you far more about the subject than they can demonstrate has actually turned up in their lives.

You might be one of those people. I certainly was, and have a lot of catching up to do from 15 years of reading. I now have some decent implementation methods methods that get from mind into muscle and start producing real behavioural changes.

Making the change 'personal'

We will use a particular method called 'identification'. This is something we do all the time when we say:

"*I am* a man/woman/coach/lawyer, etc."

These identifications – 'I' = some concept - are usually not harmful unless our conceptualisation of these roles are destructive. For me, I am a man, a husband, a father, a Christian, a coach and trainer and a lot of other things.

Identification is one of the most powerful change-creating frames of mind. Who we ARE affects our perception of our entire being and how we act. Michael Hall says "…identifying sends commands to your neurology to consider the two 'the same' and 'real'" (p124).

We are more likely to act in a way consistent with who we think we 'are'.

This, of course, has a negative side as well,

For instance, when we say "'**I am**' a failure," then we identify our one level of our selves, 'I' as being the exact same with the concept. And the effect can be to frame out any positive ideas about ourselves completely. We need to be careful what we identify ourselves with!

So if we want to create radical shifts we can deliberately *identify* ourselves with an idea and it will often pervasively affect our thinking and behaviour. The trick is to do it on purpose.

As L. Michael Hall notes in his book *Achieving Peak Performance* "once you set this [identity frame], violation will generate one of the greatest pains we humans experience – the pain of being untrue to ourselves. It leads to feeling incongruent, inauthentic, hypocritical, wrong etc."(p??)

Up front I will say I trust you will identify with an idea that is healthy for you and those in your life. That's the ecology check done…!

The Personalisation Pattern

This pattern is adapted from one in *Achieving Peak Performance*. The Pattern:
Choose a frame (idea, belief, state, emotion, value etc) that you want to identify with. This will be 'x'.
1)If you were to choose something you would consciously like to identify/equate yourself with, what would it be?
Example: "I am a business man."
2)As you imagine what it would be like for you to be x does it fit in all areas of your life? Does this personalising have the kind of quality that you want? What happens when you personalise it by saying, "This is about me"?
Example: I want to make sure I am an ethical business man, so I need to adjust this description a bit. "I am an ethical businessman." When I say, "This is about me," then it seems ok but I'll need to work it into my identity as its not yet."
3)Imagine something that you truly own, something that you would not let anyone take away from you (body parts are good for this) and when you fully feel the state of 'MINE', think about this x, and claim it by affirming loudly "'MINE", "MINE", "MINE" until you feel the sense of ownership settle into your body.
Example: I own my heart. No-one can take this from me. It's MINE!

4)   Identify yourself with the frame by recalling a time that you had the experience of being so connected with something it seemed like part of you. It could have been a toy, a pet, a town or city. As you think about this thing, NOW think about the x you desire as part of your identity. I have found completing the description "I am someone who..."
Example: I am someone who thinks in terms of systems.
Imagine how you would look, feel, speak and act. Imagine that as if you were experiencing it right now. Make it bright, colourful, vivid and dramatic. 'Try it on'. Enjoy the 'me' with this frame of mind.
5) Now notice what it's like as you imagine moving into the days and weeks to come with this self-definition...do you like this? Is it ecological for all your relationships?"
Example: Yes, as long as I confine doing this to the areas of my life where I do business, it'll be fine.

There are numerous implementation techniques around. The NLP Swish Pattern (find it free on Google) can act as one as well but I advise you to use this technique wisely. If you have any concerns, get a professional (like me!) to work with you.

One other way to kick start the process of implementation is to do what William James, the father of psychology said: "Never leave the scene of a decision without taking some action, however small."

Translating what we know into what we do is important as it underscores our entire personal growth. I urge you to study this important subject as a fundamental life-skill. Mastering implementation can enable you to become an exemplar and a leader in your field – and you can.

Chapter 7 – meaning: the cornerstone of personal development

Everything can be taken from a man or a woman but one thing: the last of human freedoms to choose one's attitude in any given set of circumstances, to choose one's own way.
Viktor E. Frankl

If you take a good look at the world of personal development you'll see thousands of CD's courses, books, DVD's and online materials all purporting to help you change.

It can be quite overwhelming: Do you really need that many pieces of information? Or is there a common theme running through all of them, a process **which, if mastered, could massively reduce the amount of time you need to instigate radical growth and development?**

Yes. And the answer is closer than you think.

At the heart of every single piece of personal development you engage in is **one** process you must do: *meaning-making.*

Every process that changes how you think and feel changes what something *means* to you.

We predominantly understand, and act upon our world through and because of what it means to us. Meanings drive us because every meaning contains something we value – in the mind a thought is simultaneously a meaning, a belief, a value and many other 'names' as well.

We will live and die for meanings. Wars are started and peace is forged because of the meanings that people give to events. Hitler convinced the German race that the Aryans were the 'master race' and that *meant* they had a right to rule and subjugate other races. They acted upon their meanings and we got World War 2.

Viktor Frankl, the man who gave the quote heading the chapter determined that *he* would stay alive whilst enduring the horrors of a Nazi concentration camp because he found a meaning to live for. He would outlive the camp and teach people on the importance of meaning! In fact, he founded *Logotherapy* – the psychology of Meaning.

To demonstrate to yourself the importance of meaning think about your interests, your hobbies. Some people will travel the world to collect stamps or buttons – while the rest of us couldn't care less! Why? Because those things are meaning-less to us.

Think of something you have achieved that you are very proud of. It doesn't have to be winning a Nobel prize, it can be growing a prize tomato if you want! But when you have something, ask yourself, "What does this mean to me? What meanings have I attributed to this?" and jot a few down.

Now think of something you don't care about. Perhaps a paper cup or a knot on the tree outside. What does that mean to you?

Your answers drive your perceptions of those events and things.

This becomes important when you think of yourself at an identity level. Try thinking of yourself as a 'success'. How would you stand, walk, talk, what would you expect from the world? And now think of your self as a 'failure.' How does that entice you to act and think and feel?

There's a world of difference between the two, isn't there? On the face of it we are just playing with semantics but the mental definitions of those words invite completely different reactions – <u>because meaning affects the very way you perceive yourself</u>. Yes, it's that powerful folks.

It stands to reason, therefore, that taking control of our meaning making processes is utterly key to taking control of our personal direction in life.

The word meaning comes from High German and means "what we hold in mind". So most pieces of personal development facilitate change to what you 'hold in mind'.

It does not matter whether you are reading Anthony Robbins or Zig Zaglar – their source tool is meaning. Even the more esoteric new age stuff "the universe will provide" changes the way you perceive the source of all things – for many it is a god or gods – for some it is 'the universe'.

Meaning is a mental process. It's not a thing. You never tripped over a chunk of meaning in the street. And it's flexible. You can bend it, change it, it's more malleable than silly putty.

This story will illustrate.

A old man in a village had a horse. It ran away and the villagers said it was bad luck. The old man said, "Maybe."
The horse returned with two other wild horses. The villagers said it was a blessing. The old man said, "Maybe."
The old man's son rode on of the horses and it threw him, breaking his leg. The villagers said it was bad luck. The old man said, "Maybe."
Then the army came around conscripting young men and took all the men in the village except the boy with the broken leg. The villagers said it was a blessings. The old man said...you guessed it..."Maybe."
This story makes it abundantly clear that meaning is dependent on context. And if you change the context, you change the meaning. And changing the meaning-context changes your experience of reality itself which just goes to show that subjective reality...does not really exist outside of you!

By now you may be wondering how you can go about changing meanings.

Well, the good news is that you do it already whenever you say to someone, "No, it's not this, it's that." As in "He's not being lazy lying on the sofa, he's relaxing and it's a good thing he can!"

You offer an alternative explanation for the behavior – and this is the start of reframing – putting another context *(frame)* around the event. To start to do this well you identify the behavior by finding out what the person actually did.

So if someone says, "He doesn't like me," you ask "What did he do that tells you that?" and make sure you find out what the person actually saw or heard.

That gives you an external behaviour – we'll call that EB.

Then you find out what that behavior means to them. In this case let's imagine that John walked past Anne in the corridor and didn't say, "hello" to her. Then we can connect the EB (walked past me without saying hello) with the meaning (which we will call IS – internal state) and we get:

EB (walked past me) = IS (doesn't like me).

At that point you can offer alternative explanations such as, "You know John has a major project on right now. I guess he was just thinking about that big meeting he has later..."

And if the person accepts it, you have reframed their reality and created a more positive view of life.

This process comes into its own when you can do it in a way that changes peoples' whole perception of the importance of their life.

If someone was feeling depressed about not finishing their writing you might find their meaning formula was something like:

Unfinished book (EB) =>(equals or leads to) people won't like it anyway (IS).

What if we reframed this to, :You have a unique perspective on life and personal development gathered from years of hard won experience. Do you want to deny that experience to people who could really benefit from it? By releasing this book you could save others years of having to go through the struggles you went through. This book is unique, and no-one else can write it but you. Look at what life is demanding of you – will you rise to it?"

So are you even a little interested in the power you could gain to influence yourself and others for the better through changing meanings on purpose? The examples given above are fairly simple and they don't always work so there are more advanced tools I have recommended below.

An easy way to start is, when you are feeling negative or like you need a change of perspective ask yourself, "What are three other meanings I could give to this?"

If you are struggling then ask yourself, "How would my best friend see it? How would [pick a historical or imaginary figure] view it? How would my cat view it?(!)"

These different perceptual positions (their technical title) will help free up your thinking and make it more flexible.

Ultimately, once you realize that only you truly control your meaning making you'll get to a position where you can say: What do I WANT this to mean to me?"

And when you can do that, you are Neo in the Matrix movies, and you are mastering…your Matrix.

Books for Changing Meanings

Sleight of Mouth – Robert Dilts (easy reading)

Reframing - Richard Bandler and John Grinder (intermediate)

Mind-Lines - Lines for Changing Minds (advanced) – Michael Hall and Bobby Bodenhammer

Chapter 8 - Three Words that kill the Human Spirit

There are three words that kill dreams. The funny thing is that most people would consider these three words necessary to make dreams come true. And they do… But as our grandmothers used to say: "There is a place for everything, and everything in its place", I think something is seriously out of place.

We are a society increasingly focused on pragmatism, on *how*. We want to get things done and we invest a lot in finding out what works. But we are increasingly a society focused on getting results by looking to what *already* works whilst dismissing the ideals that seeded them. And this can have a strangling effect on your dreams.

Why? Because ideals, and dreams built from ideals are often not pragmatic. They usually require new ways of thinking to realize. They may offer few (if any) guarantees of success but lots of perceived risk and maybe some real uncertainty. In fact, ideals are not meant to be reasonable or even practical at times. And for that reason, many (unconsciously) negate them in favor of 'what works'.

What we seem to have forgotten (or foregone) is that ideals are valuable in and of themselves. Honesty, justice – the virtues – are beautiful. Wanting to change the world for the better is an ideal, and can be beautiful. It just may not be an instantly beautiful process. In fact, it might be quite a stumbling frustrating one, but one always driven by the ideal.

Having a passion about an ideal, sadly, scares people because we often nowadays see them played out in practical form through extremism of a negative kind – suicide bombers for example. But just because the ideas of fundamentalism and idealism have become associated with terrorism does it mean that finding something fundamentally valuable – and living and loving for it - is inherently bad?

Think of how the world has <u>also</u> changed for the better because of idealism.

You could easily say that Mother Theresa was an extremist in her love for the poor. She said she was driven by the idea that every battered diseased body she was treating was the body of her Lord Jesus. Whether you agree with her motives it's impossible to deny her impact for the good.

However, I suspect if this little unassuming Albanian nun had suggested she set up a worldwide organization of nuns devoted to serving the poor when she first started she would have been laughed out of the nunnery because *it didn't seem practical.*

At what point did it become okay to sacrifice our dreams because they weren't practical?

At no other time in history than now was it more convenient to dream 'impossible' dreams. If we have a job and food we are doing better than a great percentage of humanity. The opportunities for making a living in a myriad of different ways are better now than they have ever been.

Again I ask: why would you deny that something you yearned after was valuable simply because you couldn't get it? You can yearn for and value world peace and the unity of mankind if you so wish it (and I do!).

Yes, it may seem unrealistic but some people work towards world peace, the eradication of world poverty. Yes, the odds they face seem insurmountable but they value the ideal itself enough to act on it.

You need why as well as how

Life is full of paradoxes. As you may know, a paradox exists where two seemingly opposing ideas are true as the same time.

For example, in order to be at your most <u>freely</u> creative you need to know the <u>limits</u> you are breaking free of or transcending. And even <u>optimists</u> need some <u>pessimism</u> to make sure they're prepared for things that may go wrong. As Winston Churchill used to say: "I'm an optimist but I still carry an umbrella!"

We need the 'how' – AND we need the why first (and always) if we are to unfurl and blossom the dream.This is the essence of genius - to be able to hold two opposing ideas in mind at once.

I think we are killing our 'genius' by focusing on one side of the success coin to the exclusion of the other.

I think that we are guilty of holding "How do I?" up as an object of worship. We so want results we are getting more and more wary of anything that smacks of an uncertain outcome.

Yet think of someone like Martin Luther King. Having read some of his life history it is not clear that he started with a plan for creating equality amongst all men. Yet he had a dream (!) and he was prepared to try many different avenues for the sake of the *dream*. He had no guarantee of success and stood to anger some very influential people (not to mention a great number of common people.) He was an idealist who learned how to become a pragmatist.

As Tal Ben-Shahar says in the book *Happier* "The realist is considered the pragmatist, the person who has both feet planted firmly on the ground. The idealist is seen as the dreamer, the person who has his eyes towards the horizon and devotes her time to thinking about calling and purpose."

The How may Die without the Why

However, the how may die without the why!

I started my company Living Words Coaching and Training and I worked very hard, calling lists, setting up websites, writing articles. I coached people from different professional fields and made a real impact in some of their lives. But it was such hard work, and all the money I made ended up paying the bills.

After about four years I started to feel that it wasn't worth it. After four years of trying, I had somehow lost my mojo. I started to feel listless and despite all my knowledge could not seem to recreate the enthusiasm I had started with. It wasn't until I started re-reading: The Answer to How is Yes by Peter Block that I understood the problem.

I had taken my eyes off what mattered and exchanged it purely for what worked.

I had become so focused on what would convince people to pay me money to coach them that I had forgotten *why* I was doing it.

But the moment I reminded myself of the ideals that drove me much of my fire returned.

You see, in the drive for results we have cast off what matters most. And that is *what matters*! (Think about it…)

We are fundamentally (!) driven by reasons, by values – by ideals. Ideals are often abstract though – and realizing them is in fact what most people run away from.

In the West we want answers, we <u>demand</u> answers. Perhaps that's why belief in God is declining. Because in the bible God says (essentially) I'm too great for you to fully understand. And we don't like that because the world is messy and thinking about mess takes not only effort but an acceptance of ever present uncertainty….

We want results, we want guarantees. Thus we shun visionaries and embrace pragmatism. But…

> Shahar again: "When we set realism and idealism in opposition to one another - when we live as though having ideals and dreams were unrealistic and detached – we are allowing a false dichotomy to hold us back.
>
> Being an idealist *is* being a realist in the deepest sense – it is being true to our *real* nature. We are so constituted that we actually need our lives to have meaning. Without a higher purpose, a calling, an ideal, we cannot achieve our full potential for happiness.
>
> While I am not advocating dreaming over doing (both are important), there is a significant truth that many realists – rat racers mostly – ignore: *to be idealistic is to be realistic.* (p41)

The Challenge

The challenge is to say YES to an ideal calling or purpose with no guarantee of successfully realizing that ideal in physical form. It is the challenge to say YES to something that you believe is worthwhile in and of itself. Even when other people abuse the name of that ideal, you still hold it as valuable.

In the film Gattaca Ethan Hawke plays a natural born human (made the old fashioned way!) amongst a world of genetically superior engineered humans. He is determined to get to the stars and to do so has to prove himself equal or superior to the bred humans. There is every chance he'll be caught and he's up against the best man can engineer. But as the title of the film says: "There's no gene for the human spirit."

He pursued his ideal with full commitment and with knowledge that being found out could cost him a great deal.

As Theodore Roosevelt said in 1910:

> The credit belongs to the man who is actually in the arena, whose face is marred by dust and sweat and blood; who strives valiantly; who errs, who comes short again and again, because there is no effort without error and shortcoming; but who does actually strive to do the deeds; who knows great enthusiasms, the great devotions; who spends himself in a worthy cause; who at the best knows in the end the triumph of high achievement, and who at the worst, if he fails, at least fails while daring greatly, so that his place shall never be with those cold and timid souls who neither know victory nor defeat.

You may say that living like this is too risky. Most old people when asked wish that they had dared more. Do you want your life to be counted with those cold and timid souls?

What can you say YES to today? What sets you on fire with its daring?

The answer to the tyranny of How – is YES.

Chapter 9 – broken trolley: unsound mind

Yes, I attempted to make the title sound like *Crouching Tiger, Hidden Dragon* so, staying on a philosophical theme, let me share another nugget: "The definition of insanity is doing the same thing over and over again whilst expecting a different result."

But what-on-earth has insanity got to do with broken shopping trolleys?

When you go to your local superstore you occasionally get a trolley that has a wheel with a life of its own. No matter how hard you push it forward it veers off in a different   direction. You aim it for the meat counter. You end up ramming the cereal shelves.

Maybe you can relate in your own life. You aim for a particular experience of success, head for a particular goal and yet time and time again you veer off course and screech to a halt just before you end up with egg all over your face (well, this is my supermarket metaphor!).

Do you ever wonder, "Why do I DO *that*?"

Why do I procrastinate; waste time obsessing about getting it perfect; spend money foolishly instead of saving or investing towards our goal? – and a thousand other ways of passing the time instead of staying focused.

Lacking a real answer we just grit our teeth, re-fix our eyes on our goals and try again. Perhaps we buy a new personal development program which we think will fix the problem.

I'm not biting the hand that feeds me. I feel privileged to be in a generation that has created so many amazing tools for getting unstuck. I use the best ones myself with clients as a professional effectiveness coach.

But doing the same thing again and again gets frustrating and, at some point, we realise we've been 'spinning our wheels' so the obvious answer arises. We must change our mind-set so we can stay true to our intended course.

But here you find a problem.

Because our mental makeup (which consists of what we could metaphorically call maps, models, schemata and constructs of the world) exists mostly above (out of) consciousness we quite literally do not know why we do what we do. And because we don't know, we can't change it. So we repeat our patterns.

This I call 'Broken Shopping Trolley'.

You will also have found that our minds tend to confuse our beliefs about the world around us with the world itself. This causes UN-sanity or the UN-SOUND MIND.

What do I mean?

Have you heard the saying: "the map is not the territory?" or perhaps "the menu is not the meal."

When you go to a restaurant you don't start eating the cardboard, do you? You don't read the words 'chocolate ice-cream' and assume that words ARE the cream, the coco and the ice. If you did, your stomach would soon start to let you know you were wrong!

You know that the words refer to reality but ARE NOT reality themselves. This is brought home even more if the menu has writing in another language.

We then refer to this map for guidance. However, we often indulge in a mental process known as IDENTIFICATION when we erroneously come to believe that our beliefs about the world actually ARE the way the world IS.

If you take a step back and think about this logically, it is not possible for the processes of thinking (believing, valuing, emoting) to BE the things they describe.

Why all this talk of maps and menus?

Look, if you had a Sat-Nav and it led you to a dead end where you expected a through road, you would consider it time to update the software, would you not? You wouldn't scream at the road and insist it should be like the map (or maybe you would). In any case, the map is obviously wrong.

Yet when it comes to our own 'mapping software', we tend to have amnesia for the fact that if we are not getting the results we want it could be that our map needs updating.

Despite the fact that there are six billion people on the planet with their own unique experience of the world, we MUST be right!!!

This is the start of committing UN-Sanity.

Un-sanity is believing that a thing 'is what it is' rather than the word existing as a *referent* to that thing. And when a process in your mind (like believing) gets turns into a belief which feels like a thing. And THINGS are hard to change.

For example, when admiring a flower we insist that the 'rose IS red' (of course it IS, are you stupid?') when actually it seems red to us because that shade references our memories of red-coloured items. I have given up answering my wife when she asks me: What color is this? (grin)

The reason I've written so much at length about this is that unless you get the fact that your 'map' of the world (which consists of beliefs) needs constant updating, and is fallible, you are condemning yourself to a life of slow stagnation and failure.

Why?

Because the longer you go on with an out-of-date set of beliefs about 'how things are', the more irrelevant your thinking will become.

Do you still use Word 98?

No.

I currently use the beta of Office Professional 2010 and most of what I learned from Windows 98 onwards has helped me. But if I insisted that Word 98 was the Holy Grail and nothing beyond it was worth my time, I'd miss out on some great new features.

This is what I call a rolling update and it's often essential for success.

Now, I'm not arguing that new is always better. For example, I think the virtues of love, integrity and generosity will never go out of fashion.

But I urge you to think about the above. Is your thinking in need of an update?

If you recognise that it is but you are feeling stuck you have several choices:

You could get a book like *Feeling Good: the New Mood Therapy* or if you like something revolutionary, get *Frame Games*. Both of these books have instructions about tracking back to thoughts that drive your behaviour although the second one is more recent.

You could book a free 'explore your breakthrough session' with a Meta-Coach like me. Meta-Coaches work at higher levels of the mind to create pervasive change in everyday behaviour.

The most important thing is to learn that whatever you think a thing is, it isn't. As T.K. Harv Ecker said, "The most important step you can take towards enlightenment is this: Don't believe a thought you think."

Before long you will find, like Neo in the Matrix, that, "There is no spoon." Of course – there is no shopping trolley either. And this is the start of a sound mind.

Chapter 10 - BRING IT ON to win it

Just for the record I have never seen the numerous films involving competing cheerleaders!

But some measure of this attitude of BRING IT ON TO WIN IT!; this Rocky Balboa spirit of 'get up and get at it'; this Winston Churchill "never give up, never give in" attitude is absolutely essential if you want to make your dreams come true.

I love it when people who already possess this attitude come to me for professional effectiveness coaching because either they are going places or know they should be – and are prepared to do something about it!

But what if you want to develop more of this 'bring it on' spirit? How do you do it? Well, the bad news is that the answer will be somewhat different for everyone because everyone is starting from a different point. However, the good news is that there are patterns that can help you install the right resources, once you discover what they are.

So it is possible to develop it yourself and one of the routes I know of that can really help is to learn Neuro-Linguistic Programming or Neurosemantics and apply the motivational patterns to your own self and projects. Another route is to go to an expert coach or practitioner and get him or her to help you develop it.

As for me, after 18 years of personal development work I am now strongly cultivating that spirit and the green shoots are producing fruit. Why did it take so long? Well, if it will encourage you to realize that you can start from a seriously down-and-out position – and get up – I will tell you why.

As a young man, I grew up in a household where my youthful independence was crushed out of me by a mentally ill parent who couldn't stand any opinions other than her own. I was emotionally and physically abused, and no-one did anything about it.

I was severely bullied at senior school, to the point of a nervous breakdown. My first marriage broke up. I lost my sales job, my flat, my church and my children all within the same year. As I sat in the ruins of my life, 'hard' didn't even begin to describe it.

After a year or so of being separated, I went to Wales to climb in the mountains and I didn't fully expect to come back alive. As I stood on top of the Skirrit watching the kestrels soar and wheel, the wind came up and nearly blew me off the top. At that point, I realized I didn't want to die.

Fast forward a few years and I am remarried to an awesome woman who loves God and loves me. We have a child on the way and business is better this year than the last three years. I have a successful coaching practice, and am working for the charity sector, and soon the National Health Service. (No I am not a millionaire. Yet!)

But I have absolutely been to the bottom of the barrel, wallowed in the muck, and decided to climb out. So I think I have something to say worth saying. You decide.

To me, there are several components to a 'bring it on' spirit.

- Having beliefs about what is important in life (values)
- Forming those beliefs into a relatively coherent vision and purpose.
- Dealing with fear of loss
- Learning to take risks
- Developing an optimistic thinking style
- Taking action

The Cheshire cat in the book/film Alice in Wonderland told her, "If you don't know where your going then any road will get you there". You need to decide what is important to you or you need to decide what you would *like* to be important to you. This second point is important because so many books tell you to "find what your values are" but sometimes you may not value what you need to in order to succeed.

I have had to raise the value of serving God wholeheartedly. I have had to raise the value of serving others and making money. I have had to raise the value of taking my wife seriously even when she is talking about something I did that upset her (that I didn't even know about!)

These were not values I was born and raised with: I have had to find ways to adopt them in order to succeed. You may ask, "How can I value something I don't care about!" Well, that's kind of the point – you have to find ways. And there are ways, believe me. They may not be easy but they exist.

One simple way to raise the importance of something is to write 100 plus reasons why this new activity or way of thinking-acting should become important to you. That can work powerfully!

When you know what you REALLY want you can say to any obstacles 'You're not stopping me – BRING..IT ON!"

A vision is made up of values (beliefs about what is important) and putting your values together can help you form a vision. Yes, it is a bit of a puzzle but when you have, for example, the strong conviction that people should have access to basic amenities as a right, the belief that all people are created equal, a colour-blind attitude, and a desire to travel that you might go build water pipes and wells in a foreign country. This is part of my vision. What's yours?

Don't be afraid to build your vision up piecemeal. Very few people get flashes of complete inspiration and even fewer know exactly what they want to do. That's ok. What is not ok is to settle for a life of mediocrity because you don't know your vision yet. Putting it bluntly, the sperm and egg that made you weren't selected for you to spend a life of depressed smoking, drinking and television watching.

A vision helps you discard unnecessary activities and the more you know what you want, the better you can decide your priorities.

Dealing with fear, and the fear of loss is the one that stumps most people. Most people have a dream, or are capable of dreaming a dream. But as we grow older, acquire stuff, have a family to provide for and protect, we can get scared of loosing what we have. Oh, I wasn't just talking about physical possessions. Did you think I was?

What about fear of loosing one's reputation? What about the fear of looking like you don't have it all together? What about fear of looking stupid? What about fear of valuing yourself less because you made a mistake. What about fear of what other people think?

Let me tell you something. If you feel afraid, you have a number of choices.

You can face your fear. Sorry, no whitewashing it here. I have faced myself (which is where my fear originated) after the breakup of my first marriage and although it wasn't my entire fault, admitting the parts that were, was the hardest thing I ever did. But I survived the pain, and if you think you can't stand something, let me tell you – you can because you are already thinking about it. You HAVE to stand it to think about it!

You do some (or maybe a LOT) of inner work and you trace your emotions back to their origins. Books like, *Cognitive Behavioural Therapy* or , are great for this. I recommend them often.

This is something a good coach can help with. If a client is willing to explore what is holding him back, before long he will be going forward. A coach shows you what you don't want to see, and tells you what you don't want to hear so you can become the person you truly are.

The greatest thing I learned after all these years is that it's all in your head. No, really. You may say you know that but do you really?

Successful people take obstacles as a sign to redouble their efforts. How much is that fear costing you? How many more years are going to slip by, how many more opportunities are going to the wall because of YOUR fear? Yes, YOUR fear. It belongs to no-one else but you. People do not make you fear, **you** respond with fear to their words and actions.

Taking responsibility for your own thoughts and feelings is the first and foremost action you can take. Even if you don't know HOW to manage your feelings you can learn. I've spent 18 years plus learning and falling, and getting up again. When I was younger I acted like a victim because nobody taught me that is was possible to think otherwise. Now I believe, "Don't let yourself down. You're all you've got!"

In the *Holy Bible* God says to the people of Israel "I will give you every place you set your foot". Boy is that motivating to me. Because I intend to set foot in some places where others don't think I can go. I also intend to set foot all over my mind and break down the strongholds in my mind, and go mash up (that's a technical term) any more limiting beliefs I can find. That is part of the 'bring it on' spirit.

Why should you be afraid to walk around your own mind? Get really upset and ticked off about this. It is said an alcoholic cannot start full recovery until he or she is disgusted with their life.

•Are you disgusted with being so passive?
•Are you man or woman enough to start seriously dealing with your fear?
•Are you just a certain way? If so, tough break for you – because it's not true.

After these years of learning, I know I can make these changes. It's just a matter of time and perseverance until I do.

Life involves risk. It's a matter of degrees how risky something is. It is said of Donald Trump that if he could cope with the downside of a property deal that he wanted he would go for it. How did he know he could cope with it?

Mostly with information: He knew the situation, and worked out the relative risks. Risk is not just a feeling; it's about facts as well. I have a friend who is able to cut to the heart of any situation I talk to him about and make it seem to me like it's all going to be all right.

He can help me see what information I need to go forward, and what I can and can't do if I have this information.

Sometimes you just have to decide to do something despite how you feel.

I am all for working out new and more effective ways to think but occasionally you have to leap before you look.

It may be an odd examples but when I decided to assume that people were made in God's image and therefore basically inclined to do good (despite most evidence to the contrary) it was a huge step for me. I had grown up NOT trusting people but that approach just doesn't work. It was poisoning my relationships. So I decided to leap, and have not regretted it yet. And the people I am thinking about are still the same, I am just thinking about them in a more useful way!

Developing an optimistic thinking style is essential and sometimes seems like impossibility! Here's the bottom line. You don't have to BE an optimist to think like one.

Optimistic thinking involves taking on a certain point of view: that things will ,or at least can, turn out how you expect, or maybe even better. Even if you don't want to think like this all the time, think of it as a tool to get a certain job done.

If you even consider the pragmatic value of this perspective you will see how helpful it is. Why? Because without it, you will be doomed to shooting yourself in the foot before every enterprise you attempt. So if you even want to give yourself a chance to succeed – you have to be able to consider that you might.

So much has been said about taking action so I will just quote Chris Cardell, a UK expert on business success:
"The key difference between Millionaire Entrepreneurs and the rest, is that the Millionaires FAIL more than the rest.
Why? Because they take more action.
They take massive action, day in, day out. It doesn't matter if they fail, even the majority of the time, because they're just looking for those few 'home runs.'
Compare that to the typical business owner, who is paralysed by fear and inaction – particularly when it comes to marketing.
So a Millionaire Entrepreneur is someone who understands this and is prepared to implement strategies without a guarantee of success, or fear of failure. They implement, test, review and then implement again; Millionaire Entrepreneurs are willing to do more, take more action, try more, fail more, fall down more…
then get back up, dust themselves off and start again.
In contrast, most business owners, some 95% of them in fact, prefer to agonise over the detail, worry about, "What if it doesn't work?" and end up implementing or trying nothing – simply because they're still in the "thinking about", "learning about" and "planning to" stages
What they don't realize, of course, is that they've already failed. No one truly fails until they stop working to make something a success, and by failing to do anything, they've failed in the most spectacular way imaginable.

According to Timothy Ferris in his body *The 4 Hour Work Week*, 99% of people believe they are incapable of achieving great things. All of those 99% of people are wrong, but they don't know it. If you are on this site, then you are part of the 1% that believes they can. And the playing field is a lot more level!I want to encourage you – it's ok to be human and fallible. It's also ok to reach for the stars.

You just have to believe that.

Chapter 11 - An argument for Optimism

In this chapter I'm going to present some solid reasons for adopting an optimistic attitude and some techniques for doing so.

You may ask, "Why would anyone not want to think optimistically?" Well, I think there's a general misunderstanding of what it means to do so and there are always the realists who just see the world 'as it is'. Research shows that realists might be right more often but they also lead unhappier lives…take your pick!

So what is optimism?

Optimism can be defined as "the tendency to expect favourable outcomes in any enterprise" or, to put it more colloquially, "to expect the best". So it's an attitude and a mind-set that interprets events in a certain style.

With that established, what is the value of taking on an optimistic thinking style?

Winston Churchill said, *"I am an optimist because it doesn't seem worth being anything else."* There is much wisdom in this statement. Someone also said that *"Optimism is the foundation of courage."*

Consider those two quotes. Consider that if optimism is expecting the best, or at least expecting that a favourable outcome is possible, then without optimism you might assume that you would fail before you start, or at least that your chances of succeeding are diminished before you even starts. I think that is what Winston meant. And, "He who never made a mistake probably never made anything!"

Additionally, courage is action in the face of fear and *believing* you have a chance of succeeding *has* to be an essential component to bothering to try in the first place!

So there is a cold hard rational argument for adopting an optimistic thinking style. It increases your chance of success.

Now, notice I did NOT say, "you must be an optimist". There is a difference between changing your perceived identity, what you perceive as who you are, and actually learning how to think a new way. One is considerably easier than the other!

Optimistic thinking is a process, a style, a way of thinking. Just as you learned to do mathematics you can learn to think this way. If you just think of it as learning to use a tool to achieve a particular result, it can help. You don't have to give up thinking about the worst case scenario, in fact, I encourage you to still use it – in balance!

Donald Trump used to say that if he could cope with the worst case scenario of a purchase, then the risk was worth taking!

This is because even if you do adopt an optimistic perspective it needs to be tempered with some critical thinking and a healthy does of ego strength for facing the world as it is.

You don't have to go all Pollyanna to do this. It doesn't have to be all good or nothing, everything's sunshine or rain. You can accept even 10% that something good might happen and work with it. I know that must is a dirty word amongst Cognitive Behavioural Therapy practitioners but some things are worth considering as a must.

You must eat, or eventually you die. You must treat people well or eventually they will leave you to it. Etc. Etc. Etc.

And you must develop the ability to think that things can work out. The biggest irony of all is the research on optimism done by ground-breaking, positive thinking researcher Martin Seligman indicates that optimism comes greatly from learning to limit the damage of a perceived negative event.

He said that people who think pessimistically take things:

Personally (it's MY fault)

Pervasively (it affects most or all areas of my life)

Permanently (it's going to last forever)

Whereas those who think optimistically do the opposite:

It's not personal. It's not about who I am

It's not pervasive; it only affects this particular area of my life

It's not permanent; it'll be over by xyz.

I admit, there are certain life events that do have a massive effect but as depression often comes from feeling powerless, any remnant of control you can retain will help you.

Paul Stoltz gives some questions in his book *Adversity Quotient*:

What evidence is there than you have no control?

What evidence is there that this has to affect every area of your life?

What evidence is there that this has to last any longer than necessary?

He asks a number of additional questions about how much of the blame you should take responsibility for, and for what part of solving the problem are you going to take responsibility?

The point is that if you can use these processes to set setbacks in their proper context, you don't have to over think it and collapse with despair.

The person who says it's not as bad as it seems – might be right!

You can change your thinking patterns but, putting it bluntly, if you don't think you can succeed because you've let your thinking patterns filter out all possibilities of success – then you have a problem.

"If you think you can or you can't – you're right" said Henry Ford and *"You can if you think you can"* said Norman Vincent Peale.

The optimists are right. So are the pessimists. So it's up to you to decide which one you're going to be.

Are – you – getting – this – yet? It's about perception and your willingness to consider that something that you want, might happen. It's about accepting the possibility, however faint at first that things might turn out mostly or totally in line with your values, your desires.

Chapter 12 – The number one key for managing your Emotions

Why do you want to manage your emotions? If you are reading this, it is probably for one of the following reasons:

o You don't like some emotions you experience because they are 'negative' or 'uncomfortable'
o Your emotions 'lead' you to do or say things you wish you hadn't said or done
o You feel 'out of control' in some way
o You don't experience some emotions

If any of the above applies to you, the information in this chapter can help. It works best if you are an emotionally healthy person who has emotional blips in specific areas.

If you suspect you are depressed or have had a long-term problem with your emotions that is severely impacting your life, please get professional help. It's nothing to be ashamed of and I've done it.

First, it needs to be said that your emotions are here to stay. Welcome or not, they are along for the ride and you are going to need to learn how they work, and how to work with them. They are part of the everyday process of you living your life, and no matter how you have stuffed them, ignored them, or covered them up they are like the arcade game where the gnome pops out of the hole and you hit it down with the hammer, only to have another pop up somewhere else.

So what are emotions to you? You might say 'they are my feelings' but actually they are much more than that. When someone strokes your arm or pinches you - that is a feeling. An emotion is more complex and occurs in your mind-body at the point your expectations of the world meet the world. Read that again.

In other words, an emotion arises when you get back a response from the world outside your head or from within yourself and you compare it with your version of how things do or should work - according to you.

For example, if you have just come back from a surprise party (and you love surprise parties) you got more than you expected from that evening and you may feel happy in response. Or if you just got unexpectedly fired you certainly got less than you expected and accordingly could feel miserable (or liberated if you hated your job!)

Both of these are the result of responses to the world. You also have responses to yourself - if you did something that violated your standards then you might feel guilty even though no one else knew about it!

Emotions are information about your ongoing experience of life and how it matches up to your beliefs, values, expectations, and so on.

They are not:

o Instructions
o Guidance
o The TRUTH
o Reliable interpreters of experience
o In control
The above may seem rather harsh and there are certainly cases to be made for some exceptions but, having any of the above as a dominant way of thinking about your emotions will lead you down the wrong path.

Ironically, whilst emotions are neutral in a moral sense they are always 'right' because they confirm or disconfirm something YOU believe. But if you believe that Santa is real at age 32 and you find out he isn't (sorry) then your feelings of betrayal, loss, etc. will be appropriate - given your beliefs. It doesn't mean you were right to believe he still existed...

Emotions are information purely about YOU although they sometimes don't seem that way. He made me feel that way. When she gave me that look, I felt so angry. It's the economy I feel depressed about. Even this is just you projecting onto someone else the results of how YOU responded.

However, at other times, they seem so strong that we feel overwhelmed. So, what can we do to manage or tame them? The process is quite simple and also quite paradoxical. You will need to do exactly the last thing you may want to do. You need to accept those emotions. THIS is the key.

Some people will have pushed back their chair and shouted at the screen at this point that they don't WANT to accept feeling this way. But consider this - 'whatever you resist, persists' and that includes the discomfort. It is in accepting your emotions that you are welcoming them in on YOUR terms - and that puts you in the driving seat.

When you bring feelings of acceptance to your feelings and your thoughts about your feelings, you take away their insistence and clamour because you are opening the dam on the stream of feelings, and letting the water flow again.

How do you do it?

The process is fairly simple and it helps if you have someone to talk you through it:

1) Identify the emotion you want to tame or neutralize.
2) Imagine a situation in which you last felt it, and take a mental snapshot of how it feels.
3) Step out of that (you can physically take a step back if you want) and think of something neutral - where do you want to go on holiday most?.
4) Think of something small and simple that you accept.*
5) Imagine feeling acceptance towards that fully and completely: breathe the breath of those feelings, adopt the posture of that

emotional state, and speak with the voice that you use when you accept and acknowledge something.

6) When you feel that fully, think about the emotion to 'tame' whilst feeling this feeling and notice how it changes things, how does it transform that?

7) Walk around a bit, holding this acceptance state about the lower emotion.

8) Think of something neutral again, and after a couple of minutes, think about the original emotion.

*The kind of acceptance that works best is the sort that acknowledges that something exists without having to like it:

o It's a rainy day

o The colour of your front door

o How water feels on your hand

You will find in many cases a substantial lessening of the impact of the emotion and your ability to think about the situation more clearly improves. You may want to repeat the exercises several times to increase the effect.

It is important to not accept that an emotion as existing is not the same as saying you are going to leave it alone forever. If you feel strong feelings for someone (positive or negative) at some point you might need to tackle the source of those feelings (your thoughts) and once you change them, so will the resulting emotion change. But getting a clear head is a good start.

Chapter 13 – When pleasure becomes a pain

A few days ago my friend Joe Brodnicki sent me an article on the dangers of soda consumption. It was quite shocking…this stuff is evil! http://tinyurl.com/6xlmb97

If it's as bad for me as the report says it is then not only am I basically drinking fat when I drink high fructose drinks but the caramel colour is actually carcinogenic (it can cause cancer). Add the Aspartamine (brain tumors and birth defects), Phosphopric Acid (softening of teeth and bones) and Sulfites (potential death) then why the hell would anyone tip even an ounce of that poison into their bodies?

However, I would be a **total** hypocrite if I said the thought of a ice-cool cola with a fresh-baked hot greasy meat pizza didn't set my mouth watering. And there-in lays the problem. I (and maybe we) have confused *pleasure* with *goodness*.

Our bodies are designed to produce endorphins when we are engaged in pleasurable activities but because our brain has no built-in quality control mechanism (at least our stomachs vomit out poison) we have few ways of telling whether they are good for us.

Taking certain drugs is certainly pleasurable at the time but if they're so good for us why are there rehab clinics? Hmm?

When we engage in 'pleasurable' activities our minds focus in– and then invite us to do more of them. They become what are known as 'attractors' and they do just that – attract our attention more and more.

Then as time goes by we develop habits and suddenly the things we do become *familiar* and *comfortable* which we also tend to equate with good. In his book Mastery: The Keys to Success and Long Term Fulfillment George Burr Leonard calls this process 'homeostasis' and says that it is basically the enemy of progress because our bodies want to maintain the status quo.

Avy Joseph (*Cognitive Behavioural Therapy*) agrees and his approach to change is basically to keep cheering for the new belief until it becomes 'magnetic' enough to take over and become the new homeostatic attractor ie. The more compelling of the two beliefs.

There was an interesting experiment I read about. A researcher put a cat into a room and rang a bell. The cat's ears flicked the first few times but when it realized there was no danger from the bell it started to ignore it. This is called attenuation.

I, you might say, had attenuated myself to cola, pizza and a few other things (although I am officially about two months without chocolate now and not missing it!)

To some extent it's not hard to understand why we find ourselves in this situation.

We live in a "if it feels good do it" message society and we see the destructive signs of that all around us. Please don't think I'm claiming to be better than anyone else – I can just see the signs like anyone else who looks.

Obesity is rife in the States (I think Texas was the 'fattest-state' winner according to the documentary Super Size Me) and it can only be because people are confusing tasty with good for you' and ignoring their body's signals in favour of something that's finger-lickin' good… these people are literally killing themselves with food.

Sexual diseases are on the increase almost every year in the UK (and maybe the States). Why? Because people are having unprotected sex with multiple partners or with persons who have been with multiple partners. Why? Because sex is enjoyable and is good *per se* … but sex without responsibility can and does lead to this, and unwanted pregnancies and even worse, abortions. Ask a crack-baby how good it feels?

Reading, for many kids, is no longer the thrilling pleasure it used to be. Okay, I used to be hidden under the covers with a Stephen King book, hardly healthy, but I did also enjoy the classics like Robin Hood and Paradise Lost (Treasure Island was boring, sorry!) and I know how to *learn from books*.

I spoke to a friend's child recently who seemed quite unconcerned that he never read but spent most of his free time playing PS3 (and I do like games!). A friend my age said he just didn't enjoy reading so didn't do it – he plays games instead …seeing a pattern?

I do understand – flashing lights and explosions are, physiologically, a greater and more immediate 'hit' than diving into words but what happened to 'winners are readers'? These people could seriously curtail their chances of success if they don't know how to profit from reading.

Perhaps they never got the chance or the encouragement to learn how to enjoy books. And then, because reading feels 'strange', 'boring', 'bad' etc they stayed away from it. I am not saying video games are bad in and of themselves (although I do think games where you stomp on people's heads can't be healthy for growing minds) too much of a good thing can be a bad thing, right?

And this brings me to my next point.

To resist certain pleasures because you know they are not good for you is a mark of <u>deep maturity</u> in my books. Read that again, memorise it and mutter it to yourself at 3pm in the afternoon (the time you are most likely to eat 'bad' things)!

To do 'good' (read healthy and moral) things in the face of conflicting emotions is also a sign of maturity.

This raises three questions:

How do you know what's good for you?

How do you de-pleasure your 'bad' pleasures?

How do you re-pleasure the un-pleasurable things?

1. How do you know what's good for you?

I realize in this Postmodern and multicultural society we may have wildly different ideas about what is 'good'. But here are some reasonably sensible guidelines:

<u>Sources of wisdom and knowledge</u>

Timeless books like the Bible are sources of wisdom and good principles for living. Steven K Scott claims in <u>The Richest Man who Ever Lived</u> that he got rich living the Proverbs on a daily basis. Man hasn't really changed so books that have remained around for thousands of years often have something profound and useful to say about our natures.

Parents and elders

Someone once said: "Maturity is doing what is good for you – even though your parents said so."

Your parents have lived longer than you. Fact. They have probably made more mistakes than you. Possible fact. They almost certainly have learned some of what NOT to do. Fact. If you have a talking relationship with them, ask their advice and why they are giving it. Elders are far more revered in other cultures. Yes, you may have to try and sort out the good from the bad advice but you'll get perspectives based on time and experience.

Modelling projects

In the field of NLP some people have engaged in modelling projects which are essentially psychological and physiological breakdowns of how someone achieved a result.

So, in Inside-Out Wealth, Michael Hall modelled how numerous people got rich, and used that strategy to amass over a million dollars himself. (If you are interested in an interview I did with him, let me know and I'll inform you when I release it.)

You can also model the results of people who get healthy fast. You can tell by looking at them (clue) and just ask them what they did.

Now we are perhaps straying outside of the region of 'good' because you can read The Prince by Machiavelli and learn how to hold onto power at all costs (not good) but as long as you are sensible you can find out how to do good things as well.

Biographies are also less formalised ways of finding out how successful people think. I am reading about Roosevelt and Churchill at the moment.

A rather important point is this: you **_have_** to learn to go against your 'feelings' and think about the principles you want to live by, and the results you are currently getting – you can find more information

about this in the Articles section of my site at
www.livingwords.net/articles

This may involve a complete redefinition of what emotions are for (clue: it's not infallible guidance - ☹) and my audio product: <u>Change your Concepts: Change Your Life</u> is an excellent resource for redefining what things mean to you.
http://www.livingwords.net/change-your-concepts-change-your-life-mp3-course

2. How do you de-pleasure the bad pleasures?

At the heart of all pleasures is meaning. That's right – the meanings you give to a feeling can increase the pleasure AND the meanings can give pleasure in and of themselves...

You may have heard the term 'sex is power' – so for all those people in power out there who have got caught out in their extramarital dalliances – just so you know: it was the meanings that got you intro trouble as much as the hormones. I believe Tiger Woods said something to the effect that he felt that the rules didn't apply to him. What a meaning.

There is such a thing, therefore, as a 'too meaningful' experience. But if we learn how to take meanings AWAY from the things we over-value then food stops becoming comfort (but chocolate will always be 'love!) and becomes what it is, nutrition and fuel, sex stops being power, and he who dies with the most toys just...dies...rather than wins...!

There are a number of ways of demeaning something (geddit?):

The classic NLP patterns such as the Compulsion Blowout, the Swish Pattern can work - or you can use a Neurosemantics Pattern developed by L. Michael Hall called The DePleasuring Pattern. It's unfortunately not available online but if you buy The Secrets of Personal Mastery book (**http://tinyurl.com/6f5aa2c**) it's in there. I recommend this one because if the classic patterns don't deal with the higher frames of meaning in the mind, you could just get reconnected to the pleasure or substitute it for something else. Before I knew this I once worked to help someone give up smoking and they started eating more chocolate. You can also find the Over-Valuing Pattern in the NLP Users Toolkit on Amazon Kindle for PC.

3. **How do we re-pleasure the things that are 'good' for us?**

You can use the Godiva Chocolate Pattern developed by Richard Bandler – just Google it and use it or use Michael Hall's Pleasure Pattern (the opposite of the first one).

A simple method though is to deliberately look for evidence and reasons why you want the good thing. Inititally, you may feel like you're 'going against the grain' and looking for something that isn't there but that's just your mind trying to hide contrary thinking from you (it does that!)

If you look for evidence you're likely to find it! As the saying goes – what we focus on grows and 'energy flows where attention goes'.

You can also spend some time doing the thing that is good for you – heck, you might find you enjoy running, reading wisdom literature, or dare I say it...eating vegetables...

Chapter 14 - Great idea: - but can you feel it?

I'll bet that many of us start the New Year with plans and a new sense of purpose for the year ahead. That's great, and the New -Year, New-Start philosophy can provide a welcome breath of fresh air, especially if the last one has been a bit of a slog.

If you compare the new year to booting up your computer, wouldn't it be great to have some new powerful programs to run on start-up? I'm sure you've already made some personal development purchases (like this book) or are planning too.

But if setting new intentions is like the beginning of an installation process for new ways of thinking and feeling - you'll ALSO need to install the new internal resources to support the 'programs' you'll be running. Otherwise you might be working with an operating system (supporting mental framework) that needs a processor or version upgrade in order to run your new program properly. If you like new PC games and you have an older computer, you'll know what I mean!

Well, I know some of you reading will already be planning to install some new beliefs if you need them. And that may well be enough. You can find plenty of Neuro-Linguistic Programming (NLP) installation techniques around the net or in NLP books.

However, for some of us, even when we do install new beliefs this doesn't mean the .exe (execute file) gets loaded along with them. What do I mean?

Well, each person has a learned tendency (on a continuum) towards action or inaction when they receive new information. In NLP these processing tendencies are metaphorically referred to as meta-programs and this one, listed as Somatic Response, in Michael Hall's *Figuring out People* refers to how excited the motor-cortex gets and how much that excitement gets you to DO.

Basically, at one end of the scale you have extreme pro-activity, represented by the person that would decide to RUN to Macdonald's if they suddenly felt the urge or would want to start exercising RIGHT NOW if they got inspired to get fit.

At the other end you have the inactive meta-program represented by the coach potato, the person who finds it difficult to get excited about anything nor act upon it.

The difference may well lie in the person's reaction to incoming information and our expectations of what information is for.

To me, part of the problem is that we live in an age when you can be (on the surface of it) be considered to know something if you can recite facts and information. There is a certain value in being an intellectual.

However, this type of knowing falls apart when you start to apply it to practical things. For any budding guitarist who has ever muttered, "I can play it better than that" and then been asked to prove it, the doing soon shows how much you know. You can either play that riff or you can't.

So the .exe file referred to above is your tendency to 'execute' or act upon the things you need to do. And some of us have corrupted .exe files where we know a heck of a lot but we don't DO much. So we get frustrated. And read some more.

The good news is that we can force and train our minds to re-open the route between our mind and our bodies. We can repave the road to from idea to implementation.

After all, you mentally conceived of how to ride a bike before you could actually peddle down the street, right? Every time you fell off you still knew how it 'should' be on that wonderful day when you could ride and stay on!

I'll bet your fingers know how to type but how many of you actually can recite the entire QWERTY keyboard? It's like your mind has passed into your muscles (fingertips).

Imagine a time when you highest values showed up in your eyes, your movements, your breathing. When just the thought of doing something towards your future made your physical body tingle and your soul ring with joy!

Think about what happens when you jump away from an oncoming car. Your mind creates a representation so powerful that it translates it into energy and instructions to your body – and you react. At that time the feelings are so strong that you could not stay there and ponder your next action even if you wanted too!

As you were learning to cycle you felt the motivation of wanting to ride, and you sent instructions to your body to do the movements. Then with each attempt you calibrated what worked, and didn't work, and did it again. It took time but with repetition and feedback, you mastered it.

Whether you realised it or not, you asked yourself:

What do I understand? What are the principles of riding? (Balance, direction, observation, pedal)

What do I believe? (That you could ride).

What do I decide? (That you were going to do what it took to learn to ride.)

What emotions do I feel? (Excitement, anticipation etc)

What is one action I could take to put this understanding, belief, decision and emotions into practice? (balance, push off, steer)

And you did all of this with the energy and enthusiasm necessary to push the idea into the very fiber of your muscles, mind and being. The process was extended over time (maybe months) but you did it. Imagine if that process could be compacted into a few minutes.

Above are the essential steps of the process that can be used to turn ANY great idea or principle into a felt conviction.

The process clears out blockages between thinking and doing and creates a streamlined process for becoming a powerful implementer. I won't lie to you, it does take perseverance to get it working and Hall says it can take between few minutes to an hour for a person to 'get it' the first time but after that it begins to become a habit. And the road becomes an implementation super highway!

The bottom line is that our personal development books are fantastic and full of excellent principles – which we often don't feel strongly motivated to implement.

But the more deeply you install an idea the more likely it is to stay with you in the times you need it. There is a difference between a passing thought and a felt conviction. We encourage each other to 'feel the fear and do it anyway,' but we also need to 'feel the principle and do it anyway.'

When a valued idea like, "wealth is built by saving 10% of my income" becomes a felt conviction in your gut, you'll more easily act upon it. Someone once said, "People cannot but move in the direction of their values."

Once you get the habit of installing great ideas you can start doing what I call 'a rolling map update' whereby you are doing what Tony Robbins calls CANI – constant and never-ending improvement.

And that can't be bad for a great year.

Chapter 15 - A new philosophy about failure

I, the prosecution, charge the concept 'failure' with the most heinous of crimes.

This pseudo-word has spread its diseased mimetic message across societies world-wide, and smothers the potential of millions of human beings every day. It corrupts, stifles and fills the most ambitious people with terror. Your Honours reading this brief – it needs to die.

Brothers in success, it's time to step-up and stop stroking the idea of failure. It needs to die, or to be reborn. For most people, it's just toxic – a show stopper which kills 'idea-babies' before they are born.

Let's cut to the chase. We need to stop plastering the idea of failure with mental-band aids. We need to redefine it from the inside out until it works for us, or is unmasked and killed off as the illusory terror it claims to be.

You don't need to keep un-useful beliefs - it's your head they're in.

My epiphany about this came one day, after years of suffering mild and occasionally major depression, when I suddenly realized, "It's just not worth getting depressed."

Why is this such an important realisation? Because I realised I didn't HAVE to get depressed because I was in control of my thoughts, not the other way around. And what's more, from a higher mental perspective, I realised that getting down, low, and unmotivated didn't serve me. In fact, it just wasted time, money and life.

So I decided to do my best to eliminate thinking that tripped me up. I decided I was sick to death of hiding from the concepts in my own head. It's my mind, and I choose what stays in it.

And one thing that wasn't going to stay in my head for a second longer than necessary was my concept of failure which left me terrified inside to act, and feeling like I wasn't a real man because I was too scared to act.

So I put it on trial, decided it was guilty, – and sentenced it to death.

"You can if you think you can" – Henry Ford

I argue that it's time for YOU to get hard-line with your mind and challenge your to rise up, and make a decision to only keep beliefs and ideas that serve you. Call 'time' on toxic thoughts? Can it be done? Absolutely. You just need to know how.

L.Michael Hall, creator of Meta-States said to me that for him, "The concept failure just doesn't process any more. It's a non-word."

Like the Monty Python dead parrot, it is an ex-word, it has shuffled its mortal coil.

"You can't kill a concept," you say to me. I darn well can. It's my mind, remember. What would I think about instead of failure? What if I just never had to think about that! Think of all the success focused wonderful ideas I would spend my time on instead!

Look, we have all these wonderful ways of creeping around the idea of 'failure' because we're so sensitive about it. Things like "Let's 'fail forward'" and "'There's no failure only feedback."

There's even a book called *Not Getting What You Want Is Exactly What You Need*. Failing is a wonderful thing! All great. But we still fear failing.

I believe the reason we fear it so much is because we have a misunderstanding of WHAT fails.

Our behavior is what we do – what gets us the results. And it is our behavior, our strategies for getting results – that fail.

If our thinking (which is behavior in our minds…think about it) and our physical performance does not get us the results we want – then we change it. No blame, no foul.

Simple?

Not for most people.

The issue is that sitting in our minds behind these platitudes, we secretly hold failure as something to be feared because it's not just about behavior.

Failure is not about YOU.

The biggest reason we fear failure is when we link the success of our performance with our sense of worth. Then not getting the results we want – failing – becomes the failure of YOU. And who would want to sentence their 'self' to death? Hmmm?

How illogical is that? If I fail to play like BB King the first time I pick up a guitar how does that make me a failure? Yes, my performance may be worth less to myself or others but my value…untouched.

Yet in many of our minds, doing something new means risking our very value as human beings. We have got to get rid of that equation.

When you fear failure you are actually fearing a belief in your own head. Ouch! It's like punching yourself in the face without realising it.

It's YOUR MIND so YOU CAN take control of your thoughts.

Are you man or woman enough to do so? Do you want to direct and control the meanings of your thoughts? Stop the 'Yes but' – the only acceptable answers here are 'YES' or 'NO'. You either have enough reason to change your concept of failure, or you don't. You are willing or you are not. I don't want to hear any whining.

We know it is possible to think about failing in a healthy way because we have great examples in people like Thomas Edison who said, "I have not failed 10,000 times; I have simply found 10,000 ways not to invent the lightbulb."

He also said "Do not be too squeamish… most of life is just an experiment anyway."

You've got to start telling yourself the truth. And the truth is you NEED to take back control of the meaning of your thoughts – which are rightfully yours.

You are strong enough to deal with the world outside your head and it may be uncomfortable, but reality (in all its ugliness at times) is the place you will succeed. Reality is your friend.

As John Lennon said, "Reality sucks but it's the only place you can get a good steak."

If we don't think we can cope with reality, we hide from it. As my friend said, "The soul that cannot face reality must save itself from it." We start to hide inside our thoughts, repress our feelings and create all kinds of avoidance behaviours.

But we need to ground our responses in the tangible world of everyday behavior rather than hiding away in the recesses of your mind from failure.

So how can you get 'back to reality'?

Well, dealing with your inner construction of 'reality' is the first step.

How to oust and decommission failure beliefs

So, what does 'failure' mean to you? Write a list. What do the items on that list mean to you? Ask the question 15 times until you can't ask it any more. Then you'll have the construct of ideas that make up your mental matrix about 'failure.'

Take a break, then look at it again with your white-coat scientist frame of mind?

How is this thinking serving me?

Am I playing things out in a way that supports my goals?

Would I sell this to my children?

How does this not support my outcomes?

What has it cost me so far?
What is it going to sabotage in the future if I leave it alone?
Do I still want it in ten years time?
If the answers are not, then ask:
What DO I want to think instead? How do I want to respond to setbacks, gaps, not getting what I want?
If the concept of failure were completely and utterly gone forever, what would that open up to me?

What would I need to change in order to adopt that new attitude?

By now your concept should be quivering in the dock. To get rid of it, after the analysis, tell it: "I sentence you to death. Die. Die. Die. Die."

Scream and shout at it. Tell it what it's cost you. This really does work and is actually part of a genuine change pattern.

The point is, raising your awareness of your 'failure' concept's construction can be enough to change it.

What would it be like if you woke up tomorrow morning with all your resources focused on successfully achieving your outcomes?

Chapter 16 - Increasing focus with the power of intention

Recently, I was watching a television show about Dean Potter, an American 'slack line walker' who strings one-inch thick nylon ropes between high mountainous places and walks across them.

Whilst that's impressive, you might think "I've seen tightrope walkers before."

But Dean is different. He does it *without* a balancing pole, *or* a safety harness, and the line is, literally, *slack* unlike the traditional high-wire walker. So it moves in the wind as he walks on it.

That's amazing – but what is more interesting is what he says about why he does it:

*"When I'm on a slack-line the feeling that if I slip, I die, totally overwhelms me...I'm after a feeling of total control of my life...that's what I'm after in **all** of my life...I'm drawn towards these obsessive goals..."*

What Dean has got (whether he realizes it or not) are outrageously powerful **reasons** driving him for doing what he does. He fully admits he knows that his addiction could lead to his death – but he does it anyway.

What drives a man to do such things?

This is the power of **intention**, driven by *reasons*, created by *values. Values are* things that are so significant and important to him that he can focus his entire mind into what needs to be done to get across that line.

What I am writing about here is *focus* – and one significant way to improve it using the power of intention.

Some people seem to be able to focus on their priorities at will; and some people seem not to be able to. When these latter people do – they can't seem to maintain it for long.

Why?

We're going to look at this and explore some of what we can do about it. But first, please settle yourself down and reacquaint yourself with some familiar (and maybe not so familiar) feelings.

Please picture this….

It's Friday afternoon. You're tired, winding down, and ready to chill out at the weekend. You lean lethargically over to your PC and check your email in the hope someone has sent you a decent joke.

Suddenly your boss appears by the desk and tells you he **needs** your sales figures (or substitute any other time-consuming report-type activity) by Monday morning, and it's non-negotiable.

You must do it.

You hear your mouth agreeing, and your head nodding, but inwardly you hear your voice groaning and whining, "Darn! It takes ages to do these figures and I'm not in the mood – How on earth am I going to summon the energy or the focus to do this stupid thing?" You alternate quickly between flashes of anger, despair and frustration as you imagine the time it's going to waste of your weekend putting this together.

If you work for someone else, and if you are a middle manager, this is probably not unfamiliar to you – and if not so at work, then you can probably remember something like it happening when you were relaxing at home. Someone has come to you with an urgent (to them) thing they *need you to do*; and you can remember the dragging resistance you felt to doing it even as you agreed.

Listen to the griping in your head. What kind of things do you say to yourself about it?

Now, clear your mind and think what your reaction would be if completing that one report (or other task) meant:

Significant promotion or major career boost.

An extra 20K per annum tax free. Or any amount you want.

A new house anywhere in the world you desired.

Health and long life.

Being with the partner of your dreams.

Understanding what is meant to be close to God.

What if it meant all your *dreams come true* just *because you got it done* **that evening**?

Ok, I know. Now, just go along with me for a minute. I know that no one's report is likely to mean any of those things.

But what if it did?

What if all you had to do was that *one* lousy report and all your problems would be solved?

How would that feel? What would your motivation be to do it then? Imagine.

Pause for a moment and clear your head. Ask yourself this: "Why would I do the report in the second case and not the first?"

Isn't it obvious?

In the first instance the only thing motivating you is probably the fear of getting bawled out or fired.

But in the second you've got better or **more powerful** reasons to do the report.

Many or all of those things listed are what people *value*, what they work their lives for, what they give up their time and money for.

It is the *reasons* that we have for doing things that make all the difference. It is the *meanings* we give to the events in our lives that determine how favourably we respond to them – and how strongly we feel about doing or not doing them.

The reason I told you about Dean Potter was to demonstrate that if a man can find reasons to do something that goes against almost every instinct most of us had (walking across a bendy rope 500 feet up in the air with no safety harness!) then does that not inspire you that you could find some powerful reasons to do what *you* need to do in order to achieve your goals?

There are some things in life that you *have* to do if you want to be successful and in some cases even remain solvent. There are things you have to focus on, things you have to give regular focused sufficient attention to – whether you like it or not.

You probably do know (some of) what you should be doing in order to ensure your success.

So why don't you?

Could it be because your reasons for not doing it are stronger than your reasons for doing it? Could it be that although it should be, it's just not registering on your gut-level importance meter? That you just don't feel like doing it???

What we need is a method of producing strong and lasting motivation that will see us through our good and 'other' days. What we need to do is to find a way to generate feelings strong enough to overcome our resistance AND access those feelings on a regular basis so that we can do what we need to. This pattern is based on the Intentions pattern which was created by Professor Hall Ph.D.

THE TECHNIQUE:
You will need at least 20 minutes and a paper and pencil/pen to do this properly. It would also be good if you are somewhere you cannot be seen as you may want to stand up during the final part of the exercise.
1) First, pick an activity you know you 'should' be doing in order to increase or turbo-boost your progress towards your success. Pick something that in your heart of hearts you know you are resisting. Got it?
Turn your paper to portrait format.
Write the activity in the middle of the top of the page.
We will now use this activity as a reference point to explore and create your higher and more powerful mental motivations.
2) Answer the questions about 'How is this activity important to me?'
I take it that activity is significant, right?
How is it significant?
How is it valuable?
How is it meaningful?
What else is important about that?
How many other answers can you identify about this activity?

Write your answers from left to right of the page about an inch below the activity. Basically write what looks like a paragraph of answers.

3) Take a mental step back. Well done. You've started to explore your mind set and ask questions about your motivations which is more than many people do.

Now, look at the answers you have just written. Your activity is important to you because of these things, right?

Now ask the following questions about your *answers*.

And how are these answers important to me?

What is important about having this?

And if you got these feelings and senses of value exactly as you wanted them, what's even more important than that?

Write down the answers in a paragraph an inch or two below your previous answers.

[Please go with the question and consider your answers even if it seems a little strange to do so.]

Keep doing steps 2 and 3 **until** you find yourself just repeating the same sort of answers as you did in the previous paragraph.

4) When you can't list any more answers, look at your final paragraphs and let yourself feel your response to them. It will probably be powerful. Now, (and this is important) think about your **activity** whilst feeling these feelings. Imagine DOING the activity whilst feeling these powerful feelings.

Doesn't this begin to totally transform your perceptions of that? How does this work?

The cut and dried version comes from paraphrasing the German philosopher Nietzchie, : "A man can endure *how* if he has a strong enough *WHY*" [my italics and capitalization]

Dean Potter's why drives him to do extreme things. For the rest of us, making those business calls, building that shed, and booking that training seminar might be enough to start with!

Chapter: CLOSING THOUGHTS

It took a lot of courage for me to release this book. I know I am far from perfect and can do the opposite of what I say in these very pages. Re-reading the final edit, I found myself saying a few times: "That's a great idea!" which is a sign I hadn't used it for a while!

But I know what it's like to fight from a position of having no tools or help at-all to renew my mind so I decided to share some of the insights I've gleaned from others with you. I really hope they help you as they have helped me.

<u>After all that is said and done</u> I have found my true rest in Christ Jesus, as have billions of other people.

I also have come to the radical conclusion that self-help material should be used to get us to a point where we can listen to God so clearly we don't need to use it. It's just a means to an end after all.

Life is so short. And there are so many ways we can mess it up. We humans are both immensely complex and immensely simple at the same time.

Human nature hasn't changed much over the centuries (if at-all) so those who do not learn from the past really are doomed to repeat it.

I implore you. Listen to the timeless and eternal God, your Maker and let Him guide you into the Truth about who you are and how you work.

Wherever you are, may God bless you.

ABOUT THE AUTHOR

Douglas Cartwright ACMC NLP BA Hons

Meta-Coach NLP Trainer

Douglas Cartwright, director of a small but growing Self-Leadership coaching and training company, has worked personally with a select group of dedicated career professionals since the inception of Living Words Coaching and Training in 2008.

Across the professional spectrum from Church Leaders to IT Project Managers to members of the UK National Health Service (managerial and surgical team members) he has helped people access and improve control of their personal resources leading to a more effective professional performance at work.

The company is listed as a provider of services by several professional UK organizations including the Institute of Analysts and Programmers and the Charted Institute of Communication and Print.

Douglas combines his specialist knowledge of 21st century models of human functioning and change management with a powerful focus on personal implementation.

His insistence on real-world testing of any changes made in coaching enables his clients to release their potential in the day-to-day situations where it really counts – and in achieving short and long term strategic business objectives.

His two years of professional coaching is backed by 17 years of interest in, and study and application of, personal change technology. He is a Certified Meta-Coach with a four-year rolling license renewed in Sweden in October 2010. This is one of the most highly benchmarked and challenging coaching courses in the world and unlike many courses, certification is based on seen proof of competency rather than mere attendance.

He is also an NLP Trainer and actively seeks out opportunities to use his knowledge to benefit others. He recently wrote three training modules for an East London charity helping 16-19 year olds get back into work and college.

Levels of coaching

CEO and Directorship

Degree and masters educated professionals (medicine, business).

NHS (psychiatry and surgical teams)

Project Managers in Banking

Sole business consultants

Industries

Information Technology, Business Consultancy, Counselling and Psychiatry, Medical, Ministry, Real Estate, Marketing, Software Programming.

Expertise in the areas of:

Personal change-management

Communication skills

Confidence building

Creative thinking and innovation

Executive coaching

Impact presentational skills

Interpersonal skills

Leadership coaching

Life coaching

Personal effectiveness skills

Personality profiling

Stress management

Time management

Clients say: (more testimonials at www.livingwords.net/testimonials)

Thank you Doug for coaching me through a delicate issue that has been holding me back from achieving the level of business and personal success I have been reaching for. Your coaching style allowed me to fully engage the issue without fear of judgment and then gave me the support I needed to understand and change the hidden problem. I have gained a deeper sense of my own power and abilities and now have more energy and commitment to achieve the success I want! Martin Urban, CEO

I'll be honest. When I first heard about coaching I was sceptical, because I come across a different "coach" every day or so who promises the world. However, I decided to check out Doug's work and I have been very happy with the results I have gotten. Doug takes the time to explain things, and make sure you are comfortable with what is taking place. Best of all, he does not judge you on where you are, or where you are coming from. I now have been recommending Doug to lots of people in my database. You can't go wrong.
Matt Wenger, CEO, Psychological Marketing.com
GET A FREE HIGH PERFORMANCE CONSULTATION AT WWW.LIVINGWORDS.NET/SERVICES/FREEHP (AND A FREE COPY OF THE PERSONAL POWERPACK)

PERSONAL DEVELOPMENT RESOURCES BY DOUGLAS CARTWRIGHT

Visit: http://www.livingwords.net/services/actualisation-resources

Audio

The Personal PowerPack: Confidence and Self-Esteem Building Techniques
Change Your Concepts: Change Your Life
The Mind to Muscle SuperPack
Reboot Your Mind

Ebooks

The NLP/NS Users' Toolkit
Neurosemantics for Christians

Books
Is Self Esteem Just a Big Con?

Made in the USA
Charleston, SC
09 October 2012